A BOOT UP

THE LINCOLNSHIRE WOLDS

Hugh Marrows

First published in Great Britain in 2011

Copyright text and photographs © 2011 Hugh Marrows

British Library Cataloguing-in-Publication Data
A CIP record for this title is available from the British Library

ISBN 978 0 85710 055 9

PiXZ Books
Halsgrove House, Ryelands Business Park,
Bagley Road, Wellington, Somerset TA21 9PZ
Tel: 01823 653777
Fax: 01823 216796
email: sales@halsgrove.com

An imprint of Halstar Ltd, part of the Halsgrove group of companies
Information on all Halsgrove titles is available at: www.halsgrove.com

Printed and bound in China by Toppan Leefung Printing Ltd

Contents

How to use this book

The area

The Lincolnshire Wolds comprise an area of approximately 216 square miles / 558 square kilometres. Apart from the coastal strip Lincolnshire has often been under-estimated in the past as a holiday or tourist destination, being regarded as "off the beaten track". Recently however this has changed as the delights of its unspoilt countryside, and especially the Wolds, have become better known and appreciated.

The Wolds were designated as an Area of Outstanding Natural Beauty (AONB) in 1973. They are composed of Cretaceous rocks, primarily chalk but with some underlying ironstone in the northwest and with sandstone outcropping further south, including the famous Spilsby "Greenstone". Because the strata dip eastwards those slopes are gentler and riven with glacial meltwater valleys but much steeper slopes are created to the west. The central areas are often plateau-like. The Wolds therefore present an extremely attractive walking environment that is rarely very demanding given that the highest point is 551 feet (168 metres).

Learn more about the Lincolnshire Wolds at www.lincswolds.org.uk. Many of the towns and villages mentioned in this book also have their own websites.

The routes

These have been carefully selected to give a wide overview of this lovely part of Lincolnshire balanced with an attempt to include some of its lesser-known areas. Ranging in distance from 4 to 10 miles they appear in a north to south sequence. The one exception is walk Number 10. For this we head back north to a route especially reserved to round off the book by visiting the highest ground of the Wolds or indeed anywhere in Lincolnshire.

Safety and comfort

In spite of the modest elevations involved good waterproof footwear is essential as farmland and tracks can be muddy. And, particularly for the longer walks, effective waterproof clothing and a small supply of food and drink is advisable; even in the Lincolnshire hills the weather can be fickle!

Several of the walks include road sections and one or two cross main roads. All of these, even quiet country lanes, can present hazards so care should always be exercised.

The maps and navigation

The route descriptions and maps provided should get you round the walks without difficulty. However carrying an Ordnance Survey map is still recommended, preferably the relevant Explorer sheet with its greater detail. These are useful for locating the start points but also for interpreting the countryside beyond the immediate confines of the walk. Furthermore it is always helpful to know just where you are - for example to plan an alternative route should an emergency arise!

Most of the Wolds are intensively farmed but the selected walks are well waymarked and usually well defined, even over arable land. In the instructions "turn" (left or right) generally means a turn of around 90 degrees; "bear" (left or right) means around 45 degrees and "veer" less than that. Further help is provided by a "Sat-Nav" postcode reference for each start point.

Public transport and parking

Many Wolds villages have limited transport links. A few of the walks have starting points on (or near) main roads. These generally have regular bus services between the main towns (e.g. Grimsby to Louth). However to save repetition in the route guides the details given below are useful sources of information. None of the walks are accessible by rail.

Lincolnshire County Council – www.lincolnshire.gov.uk (In the alphabetical options select "T" for Train and bus information.)

Bus time tables – www.buslincs.information or try www.traveline.information or telephone Traveline 0871 200 22 33.

Some walks begin from village inns, each of which has been personally contacted by the author to obtain parking permission for readers. Those who do so should call in and at least buy a drink as a "Thank-you" gesture. Please leave spaces nearest the inn main entrance for non-walking patrons.

Key to Symbols Used

Level of difficulty:

Easy 🐾

Fair 🐾 🐾

More challenging 🐾 🐾 🐾

Map symbols:

🚗   Park & start

——   Road

-----   Walk

■   Building / Town

+   Church

🍺   Pub

🚻   WC

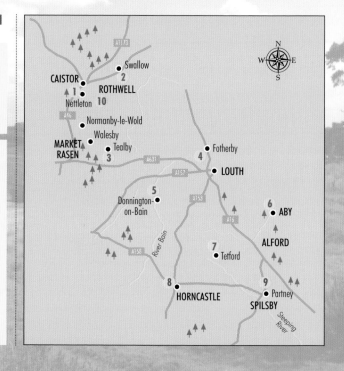

1 Caistor & Nettleton

On this walk we discover some Caistor's history before exploring field and meadow paths on our way to Nettleton. We return along the Viking Way.

The Caistor area has been occupied since prehistoric times and later became a fortified Roman settlement. Traces of the Roman town walls survive and one section is passed on our walk.

Caistor's next oldest building is St Peter and St Paul's church where parts of an eleventh century tower remain. Inside is a rare and curious object, the Caistor "Gad Whip", some thirteen feet in length. This was used until 1846 during the Palm Sunday service being cracked first in the porch and later over the clergyman's head during the lessons.

Apart from the Roman remains and the church nothing else in Caistor pre-dates 1681 when (just fifteen

Level:

Length: 4 miles : 6.5 kilometres.

Terrain: Town and village lanes and field paths.

Park & Start: Caistor Market Place.

Maps: OS Landranger 113 (Grimsby) : Explorer 284.

Start Ref: Grid Ref TA118013; Postcode LN7 6TJ

Refreshments: There are inns and cafés in Caistor and an inn at Nettleton.

CAISTOR
Roman Town

Nettleton

Viking Way

years after London) the town suffered its own great fire and was almost completely destroyed.

We leave Caistor via Navigation Lane, which originally headed towards the Caistor Canal that actually terminated some 3½ miles away. At a mere 4 miles long, with five locks, it branched from the New River Ancholme but was an economic failure as tolls were insufficient to pay the interest on the loans raised to build it.

Nettleton's peaceful atmosphere belies a hectic industrial past for the valley to the south was once an important ironstone mining area. The local Cretaceous chalk (135 million years old) contains beds of ironstone up to 10 feet thick in places and to exploit these Nettleton's

first mine opened in 1929 to supply steelworks at Scunthorpe. Peak production was in 1967 and thereafter output declined, finally ceasing in 1969. (See also Walk 10.)

The masonry of St John the Baptist in Nettleton illustrates the rich colour of this local ironstone but also its poor resistance to weathering, the tower in particular being badly eroded; but it has been here since Saxon times! The clock was installed to commemorate Queen Victoria's coronation in 1837 and was built by James Harrison of Hull, the grandson of the renowned John Harrison the inventor of the famous "Longitude" chronometers.

As we return into Caistor along the Horsemarket we pass the old fire

Caistor Market Place.

station tunnelled into the hillside below South Dale and near it the Pigeon Spring, one of the town's ever reliable springs.

THE ROUTE

(1) Leave Caistor Market Place from its lower edge via Bank Street and walk down Church Street to the church. Turn left into Church Folly, first visiting the church if you wish. (At the bottom of Church Folly - just around the corner to the left - is the Sypher Spring, another of Caistor's springs.)

(2) Turn right onto the path along the lower side of the churchyard past the plaque marking part of the Roman wall. On joining a road keep left to descend the steep

St Peter & St Paul's, Caistor.

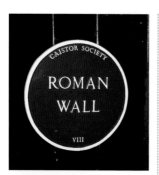

St John the Baptist, Nettleton.

Cromwell View and, keeping ahead to a road junction, then bear right down Navigation Lane. When this becomes a track continue until you reach open fields.

3 Now turn left and then make two right turns following a grass path around the field edges. After a further left turn you will come to a footpath fingerpost and just beyond this another footpath (no waymark) goes off to the left alongside a hedge. Take this.

4 After a kissing gate turn left between trees marking an ancient lane. At a footbridge cross over and turn left between the stream and a small brick hut to another footbridge. Now head over

Nettleton village.

a meadow aiming for the right-hand end of a fence near some new houses. From a gate cross the housing estate road into a lane; this leads to the A46, arriving opposite the Salutation Inn. Cross carefully and walk through Nettleton to pass the church. At Mansgate Hill turn left uphill.

5 In 100 yards go left over a stile beside an old sign "Footpath to Caistor"; you are now on the Viking Way. Cross a paddock diagonally to a handgate at the far right hand corner and join a well-trodden path over several meadows to a ramp up to the Caistor by-pass.

6 Cross to another ramp opposite and follow a path

Old footpath sign, Mansgate Hill, Nettleton.

by gardens (with two left turns) to a road in a housing estate. Turn right and right again, and at the end of that road keep to the left of some lock-up garages. Cross another road and turn right through the Horsemarket before climbing Plough Hill back to the Market Place.

The old fire station, Caistor.

2 **Swallow & Irby Dales**

This walk includes two hidden glacial valleys on the eastern edge of the Wolds. From the surrounding hilltops, as we approach Riby Grove Farm the views extend across the Humber into Yorkshire.

On this walk we visit Irby Dales and "The Vale" near Riby Grove, two remote valleys unseen from any road. Both were scoured out by glacial overflow some 35 - 40,000 years ago from melting ice sheets that probably exceeded 200 feet in thickness. They are typical of many valleys on the eastern edges of the Wolds that were cut through the Cretaceous chalk in this way.

It is the village of Irby-upon-Humber that gives its name to the nearby dale. (It may be visited by detouring from the main route at Grid Ref

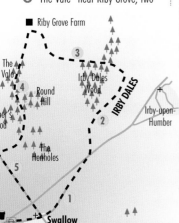

Level: 🥾
Length: 5¼ miles : 9 kilometres.
Terrain: Grass and farm tracks, woodland and country lanes.
Park & Start: Swallow Inn.
Maps: OS Landranger 113 (Grimsby) : Explorer 284.
Start Ref: Grid Ref TA173029; Postcode LN7 6DL
Refreshments: Swallow Inn.

TA191053.) Its name, meaning the "farmstead of the Irishman", dates back to the time of the Danish invasion, and the familiar "by" ending confirms the settlement's antiquity.

13

The walk begins and ends of course in Swallow whose name derivation is extremely ancient and believed to be pre-Celtic. The meaning too remains obscure but may refer to the disappearing streams in the locality; one such rises in the "Old Rectory" grounds, southwest of the village but soon vanishes again in a "swallow" hole.

Swallow's Holy Trinity church occupies an elevated position and, as with so many old churches, its varied history is revealed in the complexity of its masonry. The lower tower is Saxo-Norman whilst there is an eleventh century west door and some thirteenth century interior work. Restorations took place in 1868 to the upper tower and chancel and elsewhere in 1883/4.

Approaching Riby Grove Farm.

One significant change took place around the early 1600s when the steeple and bells fell down, badly damaging the then existing south aisle. The necessary rebuilding costs amounted to £140 and were apparently beyond the parish's financial means for the bells were sold off to pay the bill.

A local rhyme —

"You must pity the poor Swallow people
Who sold the bells to mend the steeple"

— recalls this sad episode. A fascinating and detailed guide is available.

Swallow village.

In "The Vale".

The track through Irby Dales.

THE ROUTE

1 From the inn car-park turn left through the village keeping forward at the crossroads. When the "old" A46 ends continue ahead through trees on a signed bridleway to meet the "new" A46 by-pass.

2 Turn right along the verge for just a few paces to a lay-by and then cross carefully to rejoin the bridleway as it continues on the opposite side. After 100 yards bear left at a bridleway sign onto a grass track. Follow this for almost a mile until you reach a path junction near several gates. (If you can see an exposed chalk cliff to your right you have gone a little too far!)

3 Now turn left up a rising grassy path and walk through

The "old" A46 road.

The view back from Irby Dales Wood.

Irby Dales Wood to join a farm track. Keep ahead as the views open up to the northeast across the Humber to Yorkshire and continue until the track descends into a valley with Riby Grove Farm to your right.

 4 Just before the farm leave the track going through the hedge gap in front of you and then immediately turn left. You will soon enter "The Vale" at a waymark and should walk straight through the valley woods ignoring any side paths or tracks. At the far end exit through a bridlegate and walk ahead over a pasture to another bridlegate at a farm road.

5 Turn right along this and on reaching a "T" junction go

Holy Trinity church, Swallow.

left to arrive back at the "new" A46. Cross this again and walk down to the "old" crossroads by the church. Finally turn right back to the inn.

3 **Tealby & Risby**
(Optional Extension To Walesby)

With a long-held reputation as one of Lincolnshire's prettiest villages Tealby is the starting point for many fine Wolds walks.

Tealby village has a long history. The "Tevelsbi" of the Domesday Book was quite an industrial centre for there were fourteen mills powered by local streams. At one time paper was produced here and there is still a Papermill Lane!

The village is famous for its association with the Tennyson family. It was Charles Tennyson D'Eyncourt, uncle of Alfred Lord Tennyson the Victorian poet laureate, who had succeeded to the family fortunes instead of Alfred's father George. Charles built Bayon's Manor (now demolished) in the nearby park between 1836 and 1842 as a replica mediaeval castle and

Level: ♦ ♦
(♦ ♦ ♦ ♦ if extension taken.)
Length: 4 or 5¼ miles / 6.5 or 8.5 kilometres.
Terrain: Meadows, farm tracks and some rough grassland.
Park & Start: King's Head, Tealby.
Maps: OS Landranger 113 (Grimsby) : Explorer 282.
Start Ref: Grid Ref TF156904; Postcode LN8 3YA
Refreshments: King's Head.
NOTES: The walk extension involves steep climbs and descents.

also paid for the restoration of All Saints' church in the 1870s. Much of the "old" church however still remains

(parts are Norman), something evident from its dramatically weathered ironstone masonry.

As we set out we go along "The Smootings" – dialect for a narrow passage or pathway – which it is!

Risby is known for its flock of rare breed "Lincolnshire Longwool" sheep and with luck you might see some as we head back towards Tealby.

All Saint's church, standing proudly above Walesby was left isolated on its hilltop when the mediaeval village surrounding it "migrated" down into the valley. Restored in the 1930s this ancient building creates a unique sense of antiquity and has become famous as the "Ramblers Church"

All Saints' "Ramblers" church, Walesby.

because of its stained glass window depicting Christ with ramblers and cyclists. There are dramatic views too including the county's highest Wolds above Normanby. (See also Walk 10.)

The Viking Way is used to return from Walesby to Tealby

Local dialect sign, Tealby.

THE ROUTE

 Turn left out of the inn car-park and keep ahead at the nearby junction. Then after 100 yards turn right into "The Smootings", a short lane that becomes a footpath, leading through to Beck Hill. Turn left uphill and cross the main road to steps rising into the churchyard.

 Walk round the tower, exit into a lane and turn right for

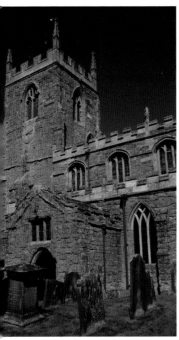
All Saints' church, Tealby.

The "Ramblers" window at Walesby.

First view of Risby.

20 yards then go left up a signposted lane. At the top walk forward from a waymark beyond a house to a second waymark near a large tree seen ahead. From it bear half right to a stile in the field corner. Continue by hedges until, from a third stile, you can head directly down towards the farm in the valley below. Cross a meadow and walk through the farmyard, turning right behind a grey barn onto an uphill track.

3 At a road go left for 300 yards then left again onto another track opposite a barn. Follow this, with views now extending to Lincoln. At Risby Manor walk round the house and proceed downhill to a cattle grid where the optional extension to Walesby begins.

The Viking Way near Castle Farm.

A Viking waymark at Risby.

4 [THE EXTENSION.] After the cattle grid turn right through a kissing gate and contour along the hillside for 200 yards before descending steeply to a metal gate and footbridge in the valley ahead. Climb (equally steeply!) up the far side and at a waymark near the top veer left through trees to another metal gate in a deer fence. Keep forward over the arable field ahead to reach Walesby "Rambler's" church. Return the same way to Risby.

5 [THE MAIN ROUTE.] Turn left through a kissing gate walking along the top of the field by a fence to another kissing gate. Now start to climb gradually leftwards uphill past a pond to enter some woods at a kissing gate. The path runs just inside the trees to emerge near Castle Farm where you should bear left following a clear path descending the valley.

6 When the path appears to split keep to the narrower right hand branch; there's a boggy section with a boardwalk. After a metal kissing gate the Viking Way bears off to the left but our route keeps parallel to the hedge on your right towards a house seen ahead.

7 Pass to the right of the house and at the road cross to another path by the small barn opposite. Beyond a kissing gate, go down a meadow edge to a road and turn right back to the inn.

4 **Fotherby & North Elkington**

This lovely walk starts on the edge of the marsh and climbs high into the Wolds to visit a deserted mediaeval village and enjoy the fine views.

Fotherby, like many places in the east of Lincolnshire, derives its name from the Old Norse language brought over by the Danes in the ninth century. From the personal name "Fotr" and with the Danish "by" ("farmstead") ending it had become Fodrebi by the time of the Domesday Book before evolving into its modern spelling.

In Fotherby itself a row of attractive almshouses line the main street. They were designed by the famous Louth architect James Fowler and paid for by Everitt Allenby, a local lad who "made good" as a businessman in London.

Both Fowler and Allenby crop up again around the corner at St Mary's church, (just off route) which

Level: 🐾 🐾
Length: 6 miles : 9.5 kilometres.
Terrain: Country lanes, some arable land, pasture and farm tracks.
Park & Start: Fotherby village. (The main A16 road now by-passes Fotherby so considerate parking is possible in the village.)
Maps: OS Landranger 113 (Grimsby) : Explorer 282.
Start Ref: Grid Ref TF316916; Postcode LN11 0UG
Refreshments: None on route. The Brackenborough Arms is nearby. [Grid Ref TF320898]

Fowler restored in 1863. Outside is all Victorian Gothic but inside Fowler's

[Map showing the walk route with numbered points: Grange Farm, Fotherby Top, Beacon, Fotherby, Fotherby Common, Earthworks, Site of Mediaeval Village, North Elkington, with A16 by-pass]

25

striking coloured brickwork comes as quite a surprise. Allenby left money in his will for the new chancel.

The eastern slopes of the Wolds contain numerous deserted mediaeval village sites (DMVs) many of which appear on OS maps. Amongst them is North Elkington, which is accessible by public footpaths and where the ancient "sunken" streets and earthworks are plain for all to see. In the valley to the northeast more earthworks (around Grid Ref TF290910) may represent a planned village extension. North Elkington probably declined, like many others DMV's, following the Black Death and the far-reaching social and agricultural changes that resulted.

We cross Fotherby Common twice on this walk, where an Armada beacon looks out across the marshland to the North Sea. When the common was established in 1764 its charter included the right of residents to take "conies" from it. There is public access, woodlands and seats from which to admire the views before returning downhill to Fotherby.

The almshouses, Fotherby.

The Armada beacon, Fotherby Common.

THE ROUTE

1 With your back to the almshouses turn left and then go right along Short Lane. Beyond the by-pass Short Lane continues to a junction where you should go right and then left uphill to the notice board at Fotherby Common. (Grid Ref TF315913.)

2 The lane then becomes a farm road and a footpath sign points off to the left where a field

> **FOTHERBY COMMON**
> AWARDED 1764   REGISTERED 1972
> Open from dawn to dusk to the general public as a recreational common. In addition inhabitants of the parish of Fotherby have the commoners right to take of the conies therein. Users are asked not to leave litter as an offence is liable to prosecution on order of the parish council.

Notice board on Fotherby Common.

path (usually marked in any crops) angles off downhill. Gradually converge with the hedge to your left in the valley floor and at the field corner cross the footbridge to your left. Turn right along a grass track, pass some woods and two dilapidated stiles before walking round a pond to find another stile to your right.

3 Climb over and proceed up the open grassy valley ahead and at any convenient point veer left uphill over the terraced fields of the abandoned village. Head for the top left hand corner of the field to a double stile then follow a post and wire fence to a corner. Go half left over the deserted village earthworks to a stile just beyond the first house.

27

North Elkington deserted village site.

4 Join a track and go left a few yards to a bridlegate on the right and then descend to the valley again down a former village street. At the bottom turn left through another bridlegate and walk uphill keeping parallel with a line of electricity poles. On reaching a road turn right. In about 300 yards, almost opposite a road junction, turn right again along the access road to The Grange. Walk through the farmyard and beyond a

A "street" at North Elkington deserted village.

View towards North Elkington.

From the farmyard leave leftwards along the access track.
You will now have fine views both of
the Wolds and out to the coast. In just
over half a mile rejoin the outward
route at Fotherby Common and retrace
your steps to the start.

Fotherby Common woods.

brick barn turn right along a short
track past a white cottage.

Go through a metal gate and
turn left beside a hedge with
views back to North Elkington. At the
field corner go through a second gate
and veer left up a grass track. After
100 yards go right at a waymark
along a field headland with a hedge
on your left to reach a 3-way fingerpost. Keep ahead now, gradually curv-
ing to the right around Fotherby Top
farmhouse.

5 Donington-On-Bain & Biscathorpe

This walk has a mixture of hilltop tracks and valley paths leading to and from the remote valley of Biscathorpe.

The two dominant features of this excursion are the River Bain and the Belmont TV mast. We don't actually see the river however until we reach Biscathorpe but the mast is clearly in view almost all the way.

St Andrew's church at Donington has an eleventh-century tower and Early English work elsewhere. The tower was restored in 1779 but had previously had a wooden lead-covered spire, which was so unpopular with the villagers that one Sunday morning they attached ropes to it and pulled it down.

Up until the eighteenth century the church was the scene of a most

Level: 🐾 🐾
Length: 5 miles : 8 kilometres.
Terrain: Some country roads but mostly meadows, grass and farm tracks.
Park & Start: Roadside near playing field and cemetery, Donington-on-Bain. (The start point lies on the southern edge of the village.)
Maps: OS Landranger 122 (Skegness) : Explorer 282.
Start Ref: Grid Ref TF238827; Postcode LN11 9TR
Refreshments: Black Horse Inn, Donington-on-Bain.

unusual custom – that of the village female elders pelting all the kneeling hassocks at the bride and groom during wedding ceremonies.

Site of Mediaeval Village

Biscathorpe

Viking Way

Boat House

River Bain

Donington on Bain

3

2

4

5

1

This apparently ceased in the 1780s when a new rector was on the receiving end of a flying hassock and thereafter banned the ritual.

The Biscathorpe valley is one of the prettiest in the Wolds with two fords where streams converge to form the River Bain. Both to the north and east of the church earthworks mark the site of the former village, though now only St Helen's church and one boarded up house remain.

The charmingly quaint St Helen's is screened from sight by yew trees until one is almost on top of it and has its churchyard surrounded by a ha-ha to keep out the cattle from the surrounding open grassland. Built in the 1830s, when there were about seventy souls in the parish, it is a riot of ornate pinnacles whilst inside is an old list of fees from the time when weddings and funerals only cost five shillings.

To the west Belmont TV mast is much in evidence. It was built in 1965 and at 1,265 feet (386 metres) in height was for many years England's tallest structure. This distinction was lost in 2008 when it was shortened by 114 feet (35 metres) in readiness for digital transmission.

Donington-on-Bain village.

At the start of the walk.

THE ROUTE

1 Walk towards Donington village for about 80 yards and then cross the road to a kissing gate on the right from which a grassy track starts to climb the hillside. Head straight uphill, and as the way steepens, pass through woodland to reach a three-way footpath sign at a track junction near the hilltop. Turn left for just under half a mile to a road.

2 Go straight over onto a continuing track that contours along the hilltop with beautiful views over the Bain valley below and with Belmont TV mast beyond. After about a mile ignore a path off to the right but keep ahead to join another track and bear left downhill.

The lake at Biscathorpe.

River Bain at Biscathorpe.

A Biscathorpe ford.

3 At a road turn left, still going downhill and cross the footbridges by the two fords at Biscathorpe, then veer left over grass to the church. We join the Viking Way here with its familiar Viking helmet

St Helen's church, Biscathorpe.

waymarks. (On the rising ground all around note the traces of the abandoned mediaeval village.)

4 Walk away from the road past St Helen's and from a kissing gate bear left down a fenced path and cross a footbridge over the River Bain; then turn right. Follow the obvious path through another kissing gate and past a lake before skirting some marshy ground beyond it. A series of stiles then follows leading directly across meadows to arrive at a road near Donington-on-Bain.

5 Bear right and keep left at the junction to head back into the village. Pass the church and the Black Horse Inn to return to the start.

St Andrew's at Donington-on-Bain.

6 Aby, Haugh & South Thoresby

This varied route contrasts the high open Wolds with the secret enclave of Swaby Valley and visits three widely differing village churches.

W e begin in Aby, first alphabetically in every Lincolnshire gazetteer! It was recorded as "Abi" in the Domesday Book but has been a combined parish with Belleau since the mediaeval church fell down in 1642.

Haugh Manor House dates from the mid 1500s but the tiny chalk-built St Leonard's church has Norman and twelfth-century stonework. Inside an information panel tells of the Bolle family who settled here in the thirteenth century and the exploits of its most famous member Sir John, hero of the siege of Cadiz in 1596 and his involvement with an aristocratic Spanish lady.

Level: 🥾 🥾
Length: 7½ miles : 12 kilometres.
Terrain: Arable and grass fields, farm tracks and country lanes.
Park & Start: Railway Tavern, Aby.
Maps: OS Landranger 122 (Skegness) : Explorer 274.
Start Ref: Grid Ref TF409783; Postcode LN13 0DR
Refreshments: Railway Tavern, Aby.

Bolle family monument, St Leonard's, Haugh.

In nearby South Thoresby the contrasting Georgian-style St Andrew's church dates from 1735. It has a beautiful east window in the Venetian style that gives an inside view if the church is locked.

St Andrew's church South Thoresby.

The delightful Swaby Valley nature reserve nearby contains hillside chalk exposures and marshy lower levels that combine to give a wide variety of habitats for both plants and insects.

Tiny Belleau village has abundant springs that produce the Great Eau. On the hilltop above them is the 1862 church of St John the Baptist containing a memorial to Sir Henry Vane (died 1662), a Civil War politician and governor of Massachusetts. Vane retired to Belleau but following the Restoration was executed for treason at the Tower, an event witnessed by Samuel Pepys.

Belleau was also the home of the Willoughby D'Eresby family but there are few remains of their Tudor manor

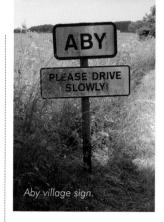

Aby village sign.

house, only a brick dovecote and a barn. Nevertheless their family mascot, a bearded "Wild Man" survives on a mediaeval archway built into a 1904 barn. He may be glimpsed by leaving the track to the right for a few paces near the modern barn and peering round the back; but don't "trespass" elsewhere!

THE ROUTE

1 From the inn turn right into Aby there entering School Lane and locating a footpath on the right by Glebe Cottages. Cross a field to a footbridge, turn right and then left by a hedge. From its corner keep ahead to a waymark at the field boundary before veering slightly right towards a hedge gap at a road.

2 A footpath continues opposite towards another hedge gap at a grass track. Now go left and imme-

The path to Swaby.

diately right from another waymark along a field edge to a stile and gate. Proceed uphill gradually veering towards the right-hand hedge to a stile at a road. Turn left uphill and take the first right to reach Haugh church.

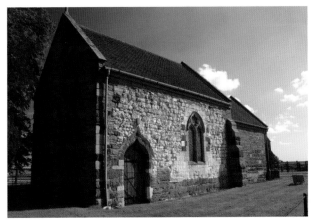

St Leonard's church at Haugh.

Swaby valley nature reserve.

Crossing the Great Eau.

sharp right over a large arable field. Keen eyes will spot a footpath sign by the far hedge, which is reached by crossing a deep hollow. Turn left along the bridleway behind the hedge to reach the South Thoresby road.

4 Turn right and in the village go left at the "T" junction and then first right to arrive at the church.

5 From a stile below the church take the left-hand one of two

3 Return a few yards to a fence corner, turning right into the farmyard and then left onto a stony track. Sixty yards beyond the last barn (there's no waymark!) go

Approaching Haugh.

signed paths, keeping forward down a meadow to a footbridge amongst trees. Cross a second, marshy, meadow (a sleeper causeway covers the wettest bits!) aiming for the fingerpost at the far side. Go along another boardwalk and over a footbridge before bearing left to pick up a narrow tree-lined path. At a path junction keep ahead and enter Swaby Valley.

6 At the far end climb a stile and pass through a house garden into a lane, then in 40 yards look for a footpath sign on the right "To Belleau". Initially the path goes uphill along a field edge but at a waymark you should veer slightly left. At the hilltop, when this large field's far side becomes visible,

Belleau's Tudor dovecote.

aim for twin trees beyond a gap in the distant hedge where a waymark is concealed in undergrowth. In the next field aim for the copse in the centre and beyond that to the corner of some woods. Walk forward alongside these to a road and turn right then left into Belleau.

7 Below the church take the unsigned track past the dovecote and through the farmyard. Go left at a kissing gate, walking beside the Great Eau to a footbridge. Cross this and a second one nearby, and then turn right behind a hedge. Go left at the field corner until you can access Aby churchyard. From the opposite side a grass track leads back to the Railway Tavern.

7 Tetford, Bag Enderby & Somersby

From Tetford a dramatic hill climb takes us to the birthplace of one of Lincolnshire's most famous sons – Alfred Lord Tennyson, the Victorian poet laureate.

Tetford, lying at the heart of the southern Wolds has a Roman road and the Greenwich Meridian converging upon its churchyard. This means that our walk starts in the western hemisphere, crosses to the east but finishes in the west again.

Inside the ancient St Mary's church is some armour formerly belonging to a branch of the Dymoke family of Tetford who inherited Scrivelsby Court near Horncastle; since the Conquest the Dymokes have been the King's Champions. Outside, behind the chancel is a real curiosity, a grave to two gypsies, Tyso Boswell and Edward

Level: ♥ ♥
Length: 7¼ miles : 11.5 kilometres.
Terrain: Country lanes, meadows, grass paths and farm tracks.
Park & Start: Roadside near Tetford church; please park considerately.
Maps: OS Landranger 122 (Skegness) : Explorer 273.
Start Ref: Grid Ref TF334748; Postcode LN9 6QQ
Refreshments: White Hart Inn, Tetford.

Hearn, who were both struck by lightening on the 5th August 1830.

At Bag Enderby we pass a large, hollow tree trunk, the remains, according

The gypsy gravestone.

to local legend, of one that the Tennyson children climbed. St Margaret's church (Tennyson's father was rector here too) had its churchyard cross destroyed by the Roundheads following the Battle of Winceby in 1643, but the stump still

remains. And nailed to the porch door is the boss of a Saxon shield. St Margaret's church at Somersby, where Tennyson's father was rector, contains the font at which Alfred Lord Tennyson was baptised and an exhibition about his life at Somersby and the locality's influence upon his poetry. Outside is a rare early churchyard cross still surmounted by a small tabernacle. How did the Roundheads miss this one? The Old Rectory where Alfred was born on 6th August 1809 is just across the road.

Back in Tetford note the early sixteenth century White Hart inn. Famous visitors include Doctor Johnson in 1764 and the young Alfred Tennyson is said to have drunk here too.

St Mary's church, Tetford.

Carvings in Somersby quarry.

Somersby churchyard cross.

THE ROUTE

1 Stand with your back to Tetford church tower and turn right. Look for a footpath sign near the lane junction that points between two cottages and follow the gravel drive past a third cottage to a footbridge. Cross this and bear half right to another bridge over a stream - crossing the Greenwich Meridian on the way! Continue to a stile in the hedge, join a lane and turn left.

St Margaret's church, Somersby.

The climb up Warden Hill.

Somersby village.

2 At the lane junction at Little London turn right along Clay Lane. In about a mile go sharp right and follow the track through left and right hand bends to reach the road at Hardens Gap Farm.

The old hollow tree at Bag Enderby.

3 Take the steep path directly opposite climbing the narrow ridge of Warden Hill. Descend the far side, ignoring a footpath on the right, to continue past woods and beside a stream to reach a green lane.

4 Turn right and follow this to the road at Bag Enderby. Turn right again and then take the first left by the hollow tree on its little green. At the church turn into the "No Through Road" on the right.

5 At the lane end keep ahead between a cottage and a barn to pick up a field-edge path that gradually curves off to the right. Just before the field corner cut leftwards across to a stile and then aim across two meadows towards White House Farm seen ahead. There is a stile between the two fields. To the left of the house another stile gives access to the farmyard; turn right through it to the road, then go left to Somersby church.

6 Continue past the church and the former rectory, walking out of the village for about half a mile to a "T" junction. Keep ahead here and in 300 yards you will find the former village quarry on your right. (An excellent sheltered picnic spot!)

St Margaret's church, Bag Enderby.

Stay on the road until just after a sharp left-hand bend you re-cross the Greenwich Meridian. Then look for a bridleway on the right.

Tetford village and inn.

7 Follow this for almost half a mile until a footpath branches off to the right. Take this and at the road in Tetford turn left and almost at once go right into East Road.

8 After about 200 yards take the streamside footpath on the left. At a footbridge turn right and when the path splits keep right again. Pass a lake and rejoin East Road turning left for the inn and church

8 **Horncastle & Mareham On The Hill & Low Toynton**

This walk visits some quiet villages in the Wolds foothills near the Roman town of Horncastle, with excellent views towards the higher hills.

Horncastle is the "gateway" to the southern Wolds where its situation between two rivers, the Bain and the Waring, led to it becoming a Roman garrison. Most of the town's oldest buildings cluster around St Mary's churchyard and the Market Place. These include an old Public Dispensary (1789) and Workhouse (1734) which both overlook the churchyard and where the gravel path follows the course of the Roman wall. Parts of this can still be found down Manor House Street and inside the library on Wharf Road.

St Mary's church is a glorious amalgam of architectural styles spanning

Level: 🐾 🐾
Length: 8½ miles : 13.5 kilometres.
Terrain: grass, country lanes, one small arable field and farm tracks.
Park & Start: Horncastle Market Place. (There is a "Pay & Display" carpark in St Lawrence Street behind the Post Office.)
Maps: OS Landranger 122 (Skegness) : Explorer 273.
Start Ref: Grid Ref TF259696; Postcode LN9 5JQ
Refreshments: Various inns and cafés in Horncastle.

the twelfth to the fourteenth centuries. Inside is a monument to Sir Ingram Hopton commander of the Royalists at the Battle of Winceby on 6th October

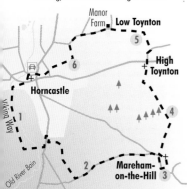

1643 where he almost captured Oliver Cromwell, and various scythes etc reputedly used as weapons at the battle.

We leave Horncastle alongside its canal (1802) where we pass the "first and last" of its eight locks. Initially prosperous the canal gradually succumbed to competition from the Horncastle and Woodhall Junction Railway that had reached the town in 1855. Final sailings left Horncastle on 7th May 1878.

All Saints' church at Mareham-on-the-Hill lies concealed behind a farmhouse close to where the mediaeval village was situated. As it has no tower the bell hangs in a small wooden turret open to wind and weather. The interior contains a fine two-decker pulpit and blue-painted box pews. The churchyard also commands extensive views northwards towards the higher Wolds around Fulletby and has a picnic table.

At High Toynton St John the Baptist church, the third on the site, dates from 1872. The village was unusually patriotic during both world wars and was rewarded (if that's the appropriate word!) in an extraordinary way.

Horncastle Market Place.

When WWI was over Toynton became one of the very few "Thankful Villages" that had all its servicemen return home safely and even more remarkably in WWII again no-one was lost!

Tragically at the hamlet of Low Toynton, a mile away as the crow flies, although only two men served in each war, none of the four returned. Noteworthy is the picturesque, thatched Manor Farm house.

THE ROUTE

(1) Leave Horncastle Market Place down Manor House Street and then go through the churchyard and St Mary's Square to cross the by-pass. Turn right along the Coronation Walk, pass the swimming

The lock on the Horncastle Canal.

pool and then turn left alongside the canal. Follow it for a mile to Thornton Lodge and join a road. Turn left and walk to the A153.

(2) Go left again and in 200 yards cross to a footpath sign and turn right behind a hedge. The path soon bears left up to a footbridge and then turns right across an arable field, keeping roughly parallel with

St Mary's Square, Horncastle.

All Saints', Mareham-on-the-Hill.

the hedge on the right. From a footpath sign in the far hedge follow a grass track to a lane then go left for about a mile to reach Mareham-on-the-Hill.

3 At a road junction bear right through Mareham village until you reach the unusual sign pointing left for the church. From it a grass track leads round to the churchyard. Walk across the front of the church and leave the churchyard over

Church direction sign, Mareham.

The view from Mareham-on-the-Hill churchyard.

a farm track before bearing left round a barn back to the road.

(4) Turn right and right again through Robinson's transport yard onto a grassy downhill footpath. At the bottom first cross a track and then some rough ground to reach a footbridge in a hedge. From it veer slightly right over a large meadow and at its top right hand corner re-

join the track. Follow this to a track junction below High Toynton, there turning right through the village to the A158 road.

(5) Cross into the minor road opposite and after the first bend take the green lane on the left next to a white house. Walk downhill and turning left at the bottom arrive at Low Toynton. Keep forward both on

Approaching Low Toynton.

joining the road, and at the first junction.

(6) At the edge of Horncastle go left on a signed footpath, the Viking Way, which soon turns right to join another road. Now simply keep forward, eventually crossing Stanhope Road and following The Becks and Banks Street into the town centre. Keep forward to return to the Market Place.

Low Toynton.

9 Partney, Dalby & Langton

Varied scenery and fascinating churches feature on this ramble in the lovely southern Wolds countryside.

To the north of Spilsby the Wolds lessen in height before their final dramatic end at West Keal. Nevertheless the scenery of gently rolling hills that surround Partney offers much variety. Note that the walk crosses several arable fields; aim to do it in dry weather.

Partney's history stretches back well into the "Dark Ages" when it was the site of a monastery, twice mentioned by the Venerable Bede in his "Ecclesiastical History" published in 731AD.

The explorer and cartographer Matthew Flinders (born at Donington near Spalding) is associated with the village through his marriage there on 17th April 1801 to Anne Chappelle the local clergyman's daughter. The event is

Level: 🥾🥾
Length: 6¾ miles : 11 kilometres.
Terrain: Meadows, arable fields, parkland, farm tracks and country lanes.
Park & Start: Red Lion, Partney.
Maps: OS Landranger 122 (Skegness) : Explorer 274.
Start Ref: Grid Ref TF411683; Postcode PE23 4PG
Refreshments: Red Lion, Partney.

The Flinders memorial, Partney

CAPTAIN MATTHEW FLINDERS, R.N. OF DONINGTON, 1774 – 1814 FIRST CIRCUMNAVIGATOR OF AUSTRALIA WAS MARRIED IN THIS CHURCH TO ANN CHAPPELLE (STEPDAUGHTER OF REV. WM. TYLER WHO LIVED IN THIS PARISH) 17 APRIL 1801

THIS STONE WAS CUT FROM THE AREA OF PORT PHILIP BAY AND PRESENTED BY THE STATE OF VICTORIA, AUSTRALIA. 1974

Langton

Dalby — Dalby Hall

Skendleby

Partney

New Road

53

commemorated by a plaque in the churchyard affixed to a boulder brought from Port Philip, Australia. Flinders actually named Australia and made the first circumnavigation of the continent.

The little church of St Lawrence at Dalby is hidden away in the hall grounds but is immediately recognisable as a "Fowler of Louth" church with its Victorian Gothic exterior and contrasting interior brick-work. Built in 1862, in only four months, it contains an ancient faded photo of its thatched predecessor together with copies of Fowler's design drawings. The nearby hall dates from 1856, the earlier house having been burnt down in 1841.

Langton village is named after the local squires, resident since the times of Henry II, and has two extraordinary buildings to see. The first is a delight-ful round thatched cottage and the second St Peter and St Paul's church dating from around 1720. Built all in brick and Georgian in style the inside has opposing rows of box pews below a magnificent three-decker pulpit. During the mid 1700s Bennet Langton became a close friend of Dr Johnson (of dictionary fame) who visited Langton regularly.

St Lawrence's church, Dalby.

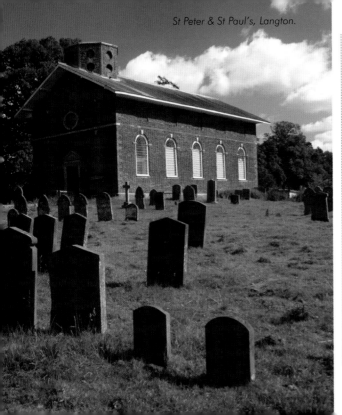

St Peter & St Paul's, Langton.

THE ROUTE

(1) From the inn car-park cross the road into the alley between the church and the Victory Hall, which becomes a footpath leading to a road. Turn right for 50 yards and then take the footpath on the left by the school. From a fence corner veer right across a meadow through a broken tree line to come alongside a wire fence and a stream. After a kissing gate follow two field edges to enter a long, narrow meadow. Veer towards the right hand hedge and in about 200 yards go through it at a stile and footpath signpost.

(2) In the next field aim for Skendleby church seen in the distance. There is a footpath sign in a hedge gap near the field corner from

which the path continues directly towards Skendleby. At a stile and field gate join a track and continue by a beck to reach a footbridge.

3 Turn sharp left here up to a stile at some woods. Walk through them to another stile and then keep directly forward over pasture to a third stile in a cross-fence level with Thorpe Farm. Continue past

a pond aiming towards a stile and footbridge in the hedge ahead. Still keep straight on towards Dalby Hall, which almost immediately becomes visible ahead. Near a fence/hedge corner descend slightly right to a footbridge, cross it and follow the left hand field edge towards Dalby again. From the next footpath sign bear right uphill to join a track, then walk past the hall and church to reach the A16 road.

4 Cross to a field gate and keeping parallel to the left hand hedge walk down a meadow to a bridle gate. In the next meadow turn left, aiming diagonally for the far corner. Cross a footbridge and follow the track ahead to a road, there turning left into Langton.

In Langton churchyard.

Langton village.

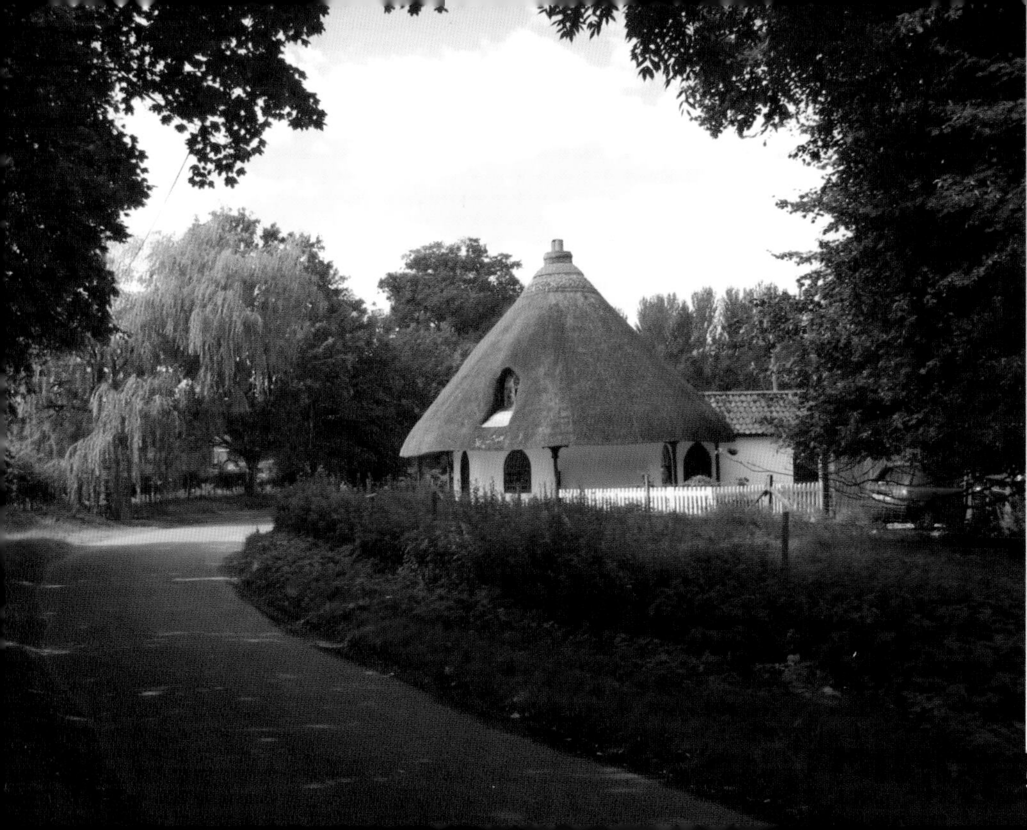

5 Immediately before the church go left into America Farm, cross the farmyard to a stile and then keep ahead on a track to a second stile. Continue past woods for half a mile and when the track bends left leave it to cross the arable field ahead to a stile in the far hedge.

6 The next arable field is a big one! Veer very slightly right (i.e. as indicated by the waymark) and aim towards Partney, but especially towards a small wood seen a "long" quarter of a mile away. There's a footpath signpost at its left hand corner where the way becomes distinct again and passes to the left of the trees onto a grassy path leading to Partney by-pass. Cross this to a kissing gate and continue along the

edge of a small meadow to another one. Pass "The Grange" and then walk down between trees to a foot-bridge and up to the road by Partney church. Go through the churchyard back to the inn.

Partney church.

10 Rothwell to Normanby-le-Wold

This walk circumnavigates Lincolnshire's highest point and visits Normanby-le-Wold, the county's most elevated village.

Level: 🥾 🥾 🥾
Length: 10 miles : 16 kilometres.
Terrain: Country lanes, farm tracks, woodlands, field paths and meadows.
Park & Start: Blacksmith's Arms, Rothwell.
Maps: OS Landranger 113 (Grimsby) : Explorer 282.
Start ref: Grid Ref TF151997; Postcode LN7 6AZ

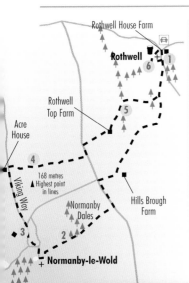

The great attraction of this route is some fine Wolds scenery seen from the highest hills in Lincolnshire. We start in Rothwell, which was recorded as "Rodowelle" in the Domesday Book of AD1086. The little Anglo-Saxon church here dedicated to St Mary Magdalene has remained virtually unaltered over a millennium; a rare building indeed.

The walk twice crosses the Caistor "High Street", a route extending along the crest of the Wolds from the Humber and via the "Bluestone Heath" road to the Wash. It is thought to have prehistoric origins, later being developed by the Romans to link their garrisons at Horncastle and Caistor.

St Peter's, Normanby-le-Wold.

There was a Saxon church here too, although the present one is largely thirteenth century, something that is more obvious once inside since the exterior was comprehensively restored in 1867. On a south aisle arch is a

The "toothache" man, Normanby.

The "rams horn" carving, Normanby.

Normanby-le-Wold, the "Norsemen's farmstead", holds pride of place as Lincolnshire's highest village, being close to the OS 450 foot contour line. The county's highest point too, at 551 feet, lies a mile to the north. (Grid Ref TF121965.) It follows therefore that Normanby's St Peter's is also Lincolnshire's highest church.

curious "rams horn" carving, which has defied symbolic interpretation by church historians, and also a graphic carving of a man suffering toothache. Across the lane a little Georgian chapel is now a farm store.

The walk's finest views are between Normanby and the head of Nettleton valley (Grid Ref TF118969), and extend beyond Lincoln across the Trent valley. Today's peaceful atmosphere at Nettleton was once one of considerable industry for the chalk hills contain beds of ironstone that were first mined at nearby Claxby in the 1880s. (Read more of this in the notes to Walk 1.)

And here, just to the south, is Lincolnshire's highest point!

THE ROUTE

(1) Leave Rothwell along the Thoresway road and in about 300 yards, at a waymark, turn right along a surfaced lane for about half a

The ascent to Hills Brough.

Rothwell village sign.

The inn at Rothwell.

mile. From a footpath sign bear left up a grass track climbing a side valley that eventually meets a lane near Hills Brough Farm. There go right and at the High Street (B1225) cross to the wide verge opposite and turn left.

St Mary Magdalene, Rothwell.

The unusual stile.

In Normanby Dales.

keep ahead beside a hedge to a 3-way footpath sign at its corner and then turn left. Pass a house, join a surfaced farm road and turn right. From a road junction bear left to visit Normanby church.

2 In just under half a mile turn right at a footpath sign by a metal field gate that incorporates a stile. Keep by the right-hand hedge to a second similar stile and follow a fenced grass track downhill to a third.

Continue beside the woods of Normanby Dales to reach a footpath sign. Turn right through the gate but then resume your original direction on a woodland track past a ruined cottage. When you emerge into a field

West door Rothwell church.

Leave Normanby (along the Viking Way) by walking back the way you arrived but this time keeping ahead along the lane. Turn left at the first junction and after 80 yards go through a kissing gate on the right and across a meadow to a fence corner. Follow the fence to another kissing gate at the next road. Now bear right uphill, and take the road towards Nettleton.

(4) At Acre House turn right by the phone mast and walk down to a gate. We leave the Viking Way here to cross the head of the Nettleton Valley and pick up a good headland path leading back to the High Street.

(5) Turn left for 250 yards and then opposite some farm buildings take the lane on the right signed for Rothwell Top. This gradually descends for 1½ miles to rejoin the outward route.

(6) Walk back into Rothwell but now look for a fenced path on the left near where the pavement begins; this leads to the church. Walk around the tower into School Lane before finally bearing right again for the village centre and the inn.

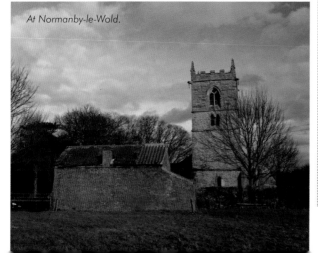

At Normanby-le-Wold.